# Lackluster Lyrics

“Don't worry about things that you have no control over, because you have no control over them. Don't worry about things that you have control over, because you have control over them.”

-Mickey Rivers

# Lackluster Lyrics

# Lackluster Lyrics

Navid Safaei

.-.. .- -.-. -.- .-.. ..- ... - . .-.   .-.. -.-- .-. .. -.-. ...
Published By NSP

Published by NSP

ISBN 978-0-578-04840-6
Manufactured in the United States of America

To the Reader:

This literary piece is a collection of compositions I have drafted over the past few years which express my views, observations, and experiences of my life up to this point in time. It is in no way meant to be a biography or depiction of my life; more so, it should be viewed as an overview of my encounters.

Each piece was written at a unique time and expresses a unique vision on life. In addition, the pieces are not arranged in a particular order. For these reasons, the tone and structure may vary drastically. To fully appreciate the intricacies of each composition, take short breaks in between pieces to reset reading habits.

Enjoy Reading.

~Navid Safaei

With my spirits torn apart,
I lie in bed.
With my eyes blurred,
I don't see the road ahead.

My soul gasping for air,
Look for a helping hand.
Finding slippery fingers,
I fall into no-man's land.

Every day,
Life cuts the wounds deeper.
This work is no one's,
But the Grim Reaper's.

I look around,
And try it to fight back.
Searching for the right,
Mode of attack.

But I find,
No sword or gun.
And I cannot move,
When I try to run.

When I gain some courage,
To begin to fight,
I realize,
I am already in flight.

It's cliché to say, "it's easier said than done".
But realize the problem, and you've already begun.

To turn our backs,
And to walk away.
To look them in the eyes,
And feel betrayed.

To know the real things
That they do.
Knowing what is said,
Is untrue.

After everything
We have been through.
It's hard to hear,
"It was the wrong thing to do."

You have uncovered my other side.
The side that tried,
The side denied,
The side…that died.

What to do,
What to do.
Going to a place,
Where the troubles are few.

I am going to a place
That is better than here.
I am going to sleep,
A place to disappear.

I smile
For the shouts,
The anger,
The fight.

I welcome
The curses
In morning,
At night.

I ease
At sounds
Of yelling,
Of screaming.

All words
So piercing
And pungent,
Demeaning

The tongue
That lashes
And beats in
horrors.

Calms
Warm ears
Heeding under
The covers.

Any word
Spoken,
Better than
Silence heard.

Over
Loneliness felt,
Any company
Preferred.

Down the fret board my hand slips,
As calluses grow on my fingertips.
Sedation sets with every note,
Deeper down as I begin to float.

Every tone, soothes my ears,
Stroking my soul, no one else hears.
My eyes float to another land,
My body escapes with the note at hand.

I am devoid, of the outside,
Just the music by my side.
Serene and free, I don't want to leave,
But I have arrived at end's eve.

With the last note the guitar string bends,
As the music slowly ends.
And I am left, with the memory,
Of a sweet, blissful Harmony.

Clip my tongue, cover my eyes, and deafen my ears.
Make me heedless to all the years and tears.
Open my mind to the life and death.
My gradual decay by your every breath.

Adapt to a new lifestyle and a new shift.
...open your arms to this new gift.
Attachment comes with the territory.
Fight the pain to reach the glory.

A simple mistake and a simple solution.
Absolve your hate and find retribution.

We breathe and continue to live these wicked days.
We seethe in the life that we set ablaze.
We feed our souls the poisons we savor,
Losing control of our lives as we waver.
But we are blind to the damage that we afflict.
It is *ourselves* on whom this harm we inflict.
But we cannot stop for we are addicted,
Though our hearts drop as our veins are constricted.
Your absence denies me your fleeting pleasure.
But your presence calls for a defensive measure.
Your feeble attempt may be too little too late.
For day by day, my anticipations abate.
'til one day, you'll be withdrawn
Never to return again or to respond.

The sun sets, while the moon rises.
Leaving shadows of regrets and certain surprises.
The darkness falls, as the wind howls.
The lost calls succumb to the demon's growls.
And while the clouds smother the sun,
The crowds below know what has begun.

Sleep tight, sleep tight tonight.
May all your dreams incite and excite.
And in spite of all the gleams and spite,
You pulled through and you know it’s all right.
So sleep tight, sleep tight tonight.
And forget the past and the unsurpassed.
For you have seen the bright light at last.
The light that will guide you past,
Past the cruel misfortunes that have amassed.
So sleep tight, sleep tight tonight.
And wake to dawn's light, goodnight.

I want to take, I'm tired of giving.
I want to die, I'm tired of living.

What do you do when you've got nothing to lose, nothing to gain?
What do you do when you've lived your whole life in vain?

There is no love when others don't love back.
There is no life when your soul is black.

To live is to love, but loving is not living.
Defining love becomes a common misgiving.

I want to take, I'm tired of giving
I want to die, I'm tired of living

Mourning a death is meaningless to do.
Induced pity and a petty life's review.

Love after death, is life without love.
A sad truth we'd rather not think of.

Celebrate life while you're living.
For regretting life is unforgiving.

I want to take, I'm tired of giving.
I want to die, I'm tired of living.

Slowly sinking in the pool of quicksand,
They were there to pull me to solid land.
Gave me the tips needed to stay alive,
Open my mind and learn to thrive.

No matter what happens i know i have them,
Humbly reminding me of who i am.
And no matter what, i'll stand by their side,
The way *i* was told when *they* lied.

Believe in miracles in the form of man.
Provided by an absolute in a complex plan.
To begin at the lowest of lows.
To learn and grow from those throes.

A magical rebirth out of the darkness of the past.
To make light of the future, something that'll last.
An illegible book of life written with tears.
Erased to create anew, all disappeared.

An extended leave, bored out of the mind.
Walls of constancy kept the heart confined.
The source has failed to keep its endless breadth.
Only 2 outlets provide the shallow depth.

Confusion stirs the mind to a dark nirvana.
Provided by gods pleasure: sweet marijuana.
The sun brings light to life's eternal leaf.
Darkness supplies the necessary relief.

Need to get away from this gateway drug,
Or give up and give in, an addiction unplugged.
Larger doses become part of the scene.
Needles, spoons, and mirrors; can't stay clean.

It is over. It is done. gone too far.
In no position to drive that car.
Keys in the ignition, foot on the gas.
One wrong move, broken glass...

Two lonely soldiers on the battlefield.
Fighting side by side with their hearts revealed.
An uphill battle for pessimists.
Can they survive? Will they resist?

The world around, seems out of reach.
"Reach out and grab it," it's easier to preach.
For her, she denies, what temptation lies.
For him, attempts, at failed tries.

Fulfilling discussions offer support.
And bring a sense of being when things fall short.
With this chaos, how long will he last?
Will she pass on an attempt, of the past?

One is strong and can stand the fight.
Will wait for the *one* to bring delight.
In the eyes glimmer a tone of frustration,
But won't give in to desperation.

As the night near, all worries disappear.
For this night shall be a night of cheer.
An absent lover must not distract the heart,
To enjoy the night even though it's torn apart.

Time and emotions will stand still,
For a moment to look at me.
My life is incomplete until,
Your eyes through my soul can see.

If my fingertips enchant your skin,
And tingles run down my spine.
Then those feelings within, have gone for a spin,
And surely it must be sign.

If lemon drops can taste so sweet,
And water can taste like wine.
Then let's quench our thirst,
Because at worst,
Everything will turn out fine.

My lips can look at you all night,
But all could be a lie.
But if your eyes can kiss my eyes,
Then my love will never die.

If my heart could somehow speak to you,
It'd be speechless at your sight.
Better then, to let it beat,
So I may dream of you tonight.

If death is the enemy,
Then life is the remedy.
These eyes are too blind to see,
What’s there right in front of me.

You have to be wrong,
Before you're right.
You have to live through the struggle,
And learn from the fight.

There is no truth
In the words that are said.
It is only shown
In our actions ahead.

May sleep render calm,
And bring peace within.
May it wash away malice,
And these thoughts of sin.

May the past teach lessons,
By our own device.
So that mistakes that are made,
Are not repeated twice.

May the future bring light,
And silence the dark.
May it remind of promises,
Of our own remark.

May our eyes tell truth,
While our tongue tells lies.
The windows to our souls,
Will prevent our demise.

May our lives prosper,
With or without wealth.
The richness we value,
Should be our friends and health.

May our death bring peace,
And calm our nerves.
The one silver lining,
That our passing serves.

I am outside,
Looking in.
Behind the glass,
I see my twin.

Use my fist,
Break the glass.
The reward after,
For the pain won't last.

The window broken,
A place to go.
From outside in,
To the people: hello.

Look for my twin,
The one I saw.
Not to be found,
I am in awe.

He is outside,
His back to me.
I take two steps,
He takes three.

I give up,
And turn around.
He blocks my view,
My eyes are bound.

Wherever I look,
I see my clone.
But no bond is made,
The reason unknown.

We stand now,
Face to face.
Just standing there,
Nothing takes place.

I stand here,
Stiff as stone.
With my twin,
But I am alone.

I am what I am.
But I am not a man.
I do what I can.
But I am where I began.

I want a change.
But what should I be?
All I know is
I can't be me.

Down my cheeks flow a thousand tears.
With them fall ten thousand fears.
And though my worries don't disappear.
I learn to cope and to persevere.

I have lost the will, the will to go on.
I lay here with my ego torn.
Asking myself shall I quit?
If I try harder will I make it?

Is there any point to this?
Does a finish line even exist?
I've done this for so many years.
Then suddenly...my mind clears.

...I've done this for so many years!
I cannot quit as the end nears!
What the hell was I thinking about?
A temporary moment of doubt.

I have come all this way.
I can feel my frets allay.
I will break away from these chains.
And keep the blood coursing through my veins.

Because the future lies ahead.
Exactly like my friends have said.

Hearing voices,
Slam a fist in the mirror.
Wrong choices,
The whispers grow nearer.

Specified advice,
Commit deeds of hate.
Perform twice,
If your emotions abate.

Thick tension,
The reaction of disgust.
Lost attention,
Issue of broken trust.

Demonic grins,
Hide a truthful lust.
Regretful sins,
Of a life unjust.

Ties seldom reconnect.
Broken if a link is incorrect.
Ties can be made to a knot.
By making lies and getting caught.

Ties require a sync of two.
Budding off a closeness that grew.
Ties are fragile, can be pulled apart.
If the first knot is not taught.

Ties made with different ropes.
A bond that has no limited scope.
A tie undone can be made again.
To be stronger than it was back then.

Around the neck,
A tie can kill.
Around the heart,
Emotions are still.

A tie is a tie and we are ropes,
Bound together by each others' hopes.

Let the rain fall and pierce the skin.
And seep in deep to cleanse of sin.
Understand the love behind the hate.
The drama of love, our destined fate.

Let yourself go and enjoy the new.
Look at your “friends” from a different view.
Learn the truth behind the who is who.
Become closer with the ones you “knew”.

Take a second to look at the past.
And realize it’s gone by so fast.
Now take a minute to look ahead.
In a blink of an eye, we'll all be wed.

Life is too short to put it on hold.
Before we know it we'll all be old.
And all the things we want to do,
Will be the things we never got to do.

Every raindrop is an opportunity from above.
Falls to the ground to be taken advantage of.
Look at the window and watch the time fly by.
Enjoy every moment and don't ask why.

An attached heart,
Keeps the body bound.
Tied to a constant,
One's rebound.

Hard to let go,
And set yourself free.
Doing the right thing,
Is not so easy.

On the other side,
Sits a helpless beast.
To scavenge on the leftovers,
Of love's feast.

A true emotion,
From an intricate mess.
But would a freed path,
Lead to a "yes"?

Times tried and failed,
Breaks the spirit.
Loneliness,
Why must I fear it?

The numbers add up,
But the answer is wrong.
Need to find a place,
Where I belong.

Repose to isolation,
I have become satisfied with loneliness inside.
Numb to love's sensation,
I scatter the ashes of my heart denied.

Habits prevail,
An exhausted cloak for an imminent subversion.
The routine stale,
Thirsting for the word in a meaningful conversation.

Lackluster Lackluster.
I muster the will,
To satisfy the needs,
For your lyrical thrill.

Lackluster Lackluster.
I heed the call,
To deliver my message,
To you all.

Lackluster Lackluster.
But you've lost your way,
Drowning in the words,
Of what I have to say.

Lackluster Lackluster.
My words are stale.
Best close your eyes,
And read this in ⠃⠗⠁⠊⠇⠇⠑

Lackluster Lackluster.
My words are satiric.
Read by an amateur,
As a lackluster lyric.

Lackluster Lackluster.
I will say no more!
Quench yourselves,
You pentameter whores.

End

# Lackluster Lyrics

Navid Safaei

.-.. .- -.-. -.- .-.. ..- ... - . .-.   .-.. -.-- .-. .. -.-. ...

“Procrastination isn't the problem, it's the solution. So procrastinate now, don't put it off.”

-Ellen DeGeneres

I want to thank everyone who has inspired and encouraged me in my life; especially my mom, dad, and brother. For these people I hold an immense feeling of respect and appreciation. Thank you.

~Navid

www.ingramcontent.com/pod-product-compliance
Ingram Content Group UK Ltd.
Pitfield, Milton Keynes, MK11 3LW, UK
UKHW041833200726
13854UKWH00003BA/1114